STEVIE

For Sheila

STEVIE

A Play
by
HUGH WHITEMORE

from the life and work of
STEVIE SMITH

AMBER LANE PRESS

All rights whatsoever in this play are strictly
reserved and application for professional
performance should be made before rehearsal to:

Margaret Ramsay Ltd.
14a Goodwin's Court
St. Martin's Lane
London WC2N 4LL

Application for amateur performance should be
made before rehearsal to:

Samuel French Ltd.
52 Fitzroy Street
London W1P 6JR

No performance may be given unless a licence
has been obtained.

First published in 1977 by
Samuel French Ltd.

This edition published in 1984 by
Amber Lane Press Ltd.
9 Middle Way
Oxford OX2 7LH

Typesetting and page make-up by
Midas Publishing Services Ltd., Oxford

Printed in Great Britain by
Cotswold Press Ltd., Oxford

All the passages from the writings of Stevie Smith quoted
in this play are the copyright of her executor, James
MacGibbon. The poetry is taken from *The Collected Poems of
Stevie Smith*, published by Allen Lane (London, 1975) and the
prose passages from her novels published by the Virago Press
and from *Ivy and Stevie* by Kay Dick, published by Duckworth
(London, 1971).

ISBN 0 906399 50 5

FOREWORD

When I was a student in the late 1950s, I picked up a second-hand copy of *Novel On Yellow Paper* from a bookstall in Cambridge Circus. I was entranced and fascinated. I discovered that the author, Stevie Smith, had also written several volumes of poetry; I read these with equal delight. Years later I saw her interviewed on television by Jonathan Miller; she wept, I remember, as she spoke of her mother's death. This frail, fringed, rather spiky woman made a deep impression on me. And then, one afternoon, I suddenly had the idea of writing a play called STEVIE; it would take place in the sitting-room of her house in Palmer's Green and there would be three characters: Stevie, her beloved Lion Aunt and a man to play several supporting roles. The idea for the play fell into my mind, plop, fully formed and ready to go. The trouble was, almost all of Stevie's work was out of print (this was in 1974, just three years after her death), there was no biography, and scarcely any available information about her. She had virtually disappeared. But I was determined that the play should be written and thus embarked on a lengthy hunt-the-poet campaign. I wrote to a number of people who I knew had been friends or had had some association with her. They responded most generously and I was showered with memories and anecdotes that brought Stevie to life in a remarkable way. A great many of these stories I managed to incorporate into the play but some remained, unused, in my notebooks. The purpose of this brief foreword is to preserve just a few of the stories that seem too good not to share.

One of the first people I went to see was the distinguished radio producer, Douglas Cleverdon, the man who commissioned Dylan Thomas to write *Under Milk Wood*. Cleverdon had produced many programmes of Stevie's poetry and knew her well. They would sometimes dine together at the Cleverdons' house in Islington and Stevie expressed a lively appreciation of Mrs Cleverdon's cooking: 'It makes such a lovely change from custard and warm cake.' But water-ice did not meet with her approval: 'It's like eating a cracked puddle,' she said. At one memorable dinner party the Cleverdons played host to Stevie and John Betjeman, who became engrossed in an animated conversation about their love of hymn tunes. 'Do you know this one?' Betjeman would say, singing a few bars. 'Oh, yes!' Stevie's response was always enthusiastic. 'But I think this one is much, much better,' and off she would go, singing away in her inimitable tuneless drone. The third guest, John Wells, was understandably struck dumb with amazement. Cleverdon spoke of Stevie's attitude to children; she liked them, but only when they were kept firmly under control. He recalled a visit to the Tate Gallery to see a surrealist exhibition. Among the other visitors was a young woman with a baby strapped to her back in papoose-style. The baby was yelling relentlessly — 'Eighteen months old and already odious'. Stevie became more and more irritable; eventually she drew closer and, taking care that the mother could not see her, pulled horrendous faces at the bawling child. 'It was her way of retaliating,' said Cleverdon. He also told me a little rhyme that Stevie found especially amusing:

> Uncle George and Auntie Mabel
> Fainted at the breakfast table.
> Children, let this be a warning:
> Not to do it in the morning.

Patrick Garland produced an anthology of Stevie's poetry for the BBC television programme, *Monitor,* and he kindly let me listen to tape-recordings of some informal conversations he had had with Stevie. My favourite passage concerns Thomas de Quincey and his addiction to opium; Stevie relates the episode with enormous zest, punctuating the story with bursts of gurgling laughter:

' ...he was knocking back about a pint of laudanum a day — having no effect. And then he borrowed Wordsworth's cottage, you see, in the Lake District and one day an extraordinary thing happened. This Malay came to the door and — er — in the Lake District it's the last thing you would expect, you see, and the Malay said to him (*She laughs.*) — "Have (*Laughter.*) have you — (*Laughter.*) have you by chance any opium?" (*Laughter.*) And de Quincey gave him a piece of opium as long as a walking stick and the Malay just broke it up and ate (*Laughter.*) it (*Laughter.*) all. (*Laughter.*) I think he quite expected him to drop dead on the doorstep. Not at all. It didn't make the slightest bit of difference to him; off he went. He was going to Liverpool at the time and off he went, you know, happy as a lark. I daresay it would have killed an army practically, but he was so immune to it, so addicted to it, you see, by that time, that the Malay could take any quantity. Well — de Quincey practically got to the same state.'

Stevie and Garland also talked about the ancient Greeks, about their drama and about their gods, whom Stevie regarded with a deep distaste: 'They're so frivolous. The gods are what the Edwardian upper class used to be in England. They had privilege but no responsibilities. Any cheek from the lower orders and down they came like a ton of bricks!'

Of course not all of Stevie's friends came from the literary world; as she said, 'Most of my friends — well, they're just friends, you know, I don't really know what they are; they're sort of married and have children; their husbands are barristers or something like that, lawyers, civil servants. I wouldn't say that I had a tremendous literary acquaintance.' And it was from these non-literary friends that I gained some particularly interesting — and surprising — insights into Stevie's life and character.

'She left her money to the NSPCC because she was only too aware of what an unhappy childhood could be. She didn't want children of her own, but, in a curious way, she identified with children.'

'She liked clothes and took an interest in fashion. In the early sixties, when boutiques sprang up all over Kensington and Chelsea, Stevie bought dresses from two of the most fashionable shops — Bus Stop and Biba's. She had great poise.'

'I was walking with Stevie at the seaside. The tide had gone out and there was a wide expanse of beach. And we walked and we walked and we walked across the sands towards the distant sea, and when we finally saw it Stevie was overjoyed. She tore off her clothes and ran into the water. She had such dark skin: a little brown body running into the sea.'

'She loved Cocteau's film *Orphée* — but from it she developed a phobia of travelling on tube trains.'

'As you know, she lived in a small semi-detached house in the suburbs. One day, some advertising people came to her street; it was part of a publicity campaign for 'Fairy Snow' washing powder, and there was an actress dressed up in some sort of fanciful costume. Well, Stevie never watched television, she had never seen the commercials, and so she knew nothing about it. When the advertising people rang her front door bell, Stevie stared at them, simply amazed. She couldn't imagine what a Fairy Queen was doing in Palmers Green.'

'She went to stay with some friends near the Lincolnshire marshes. Late one afternoon she went for a very long walk. It was getting dark and misty. Suddenly she saw a figure standing ahead of her in the dusk. It was a ferryman who rowed people across the fens. Stevie didn't know who he was and was understandably frightened. She stared through the mist at the man and his boat. 'Can I row you across?' he asked. 'Oh no, my friends are still on this side,' she said fearfully, as if it was the Styx and not the fens that lay before her.'

Stevie's preoccupation with death is, of course, well-known and well-documented. 'Shall I give it a capital D or not?' she asked Neville Braybrooke. 'Death will be absolutely marvellous. The power and the glory — I cannot wait.'

The composer Elisabeth Lutyens recalled some sharp, and not always attractive, memories of Stevie: 'She had a difficult, demanding nature; she kept bickering like a child.' Miss Lutyens spoke of a trip to Fenwick's, the department store in Bond Street. She and Stevie decided to have a snack in the restaurant; Stevie ordered tea, but Elisabeth Lutyens wanted coffee. Stevie flew into a childlike rage: 'Why must you be so difficult? Why can't you have tea like me?' 'She completely ignored the fact that it was perfectly easy to order both,' said Miss Lutyens. Another story concerned Stevie's friendship with Betty Miller, mother of Jonathan. The two women had been friends for some years, and Stevie went with the Millers for a seaside holiday to Swanage. On her return, Stevie wrote a particularly savage and wounding story about the holiday. The piece was published. The two women never spoke again. Elisabeth Lutyens also remembered a stroll with Stevie through Greenwich Park. Miss Lutyens' daughter, who went with them, was wearing sunglasses. Stevie disapproved. 'You shouldn't wear sunglasses, dear, your eyes will fade.' Miss Lutyens' daughter described Stevie as a 'funny little creature, a curious little creature.' Her mother's description was crueller and more precise: 'long nose, plain, appalling and, in later years, dyed hair that stuck out like straw.'

Eric Walter White became a friend of Stevie when he invited her to become a member of the Arts Council Poetry panel. It was shortly after this that she received the Queen's Gold Medal for Poetry; although the honour delighted her, Stevie was oddly concerned about the arrangements for refreshments at the palace: 'Will they give me lunch?' she asked Eric Walter White on the telephone. 'Will they give me coffee or anything?' This preoccupation with food resulted in Eric Walter White and Cecil Day Lewis organising the celebratory meal at 'L'Epicure' that is described in the play.

By this time Stevie's life was drawing to a close. A number of people, particularly James MacGibbon and John Guest, told me sad stories of her declining days in a West Country hospital. But it is, I think, Eric Walter White's poem, 'Farewell to Stevie', that provides the most touching personal tribute to this remarkable and oddly endearing woman.

The last time I saw you was in the stuffy church hall.
Each word you half spoke, half sang,
Dropped like a pebble
Into a quiet pool of silence,
Making a submarine cairn by accretion —
Your poem, your thing.
And the concentric ripples grew wider,
Overlapping each other before dying away.

After the reading you came up to me with a reproachful air.
— Eric, you were asleep!
— Stevie, I protest. I wasn't.
— I could see you at the end of the row. Your eyes were closed.
— The better to listen. I heard every word.
— Your head nodded.
— In time with your A and M chanting.
— Darling, as I looked at you, I couldn't help thinking of those oysters.
— Ah! So you've not forgotten?
— What a luncheon party! Norah in that lovely red hat; Cecil looking like the Poet Laureate; and you ordering all those oysters, which took so long to arrive!
— It was maddening, Stevie, especially as you had such an appetite after the investiture.

— They offered no refreshment at the Palace, not even a glass of
     swéet sherry.
— But you got your gold medal.

I still see the quick flick of your smile. But now,
Thinking of the frightened way it went out,
I wonder if you were really smiling at all.
They say that shortly afterwards,
As you lay speechless on your sick bed,
You asked by signs for pencil and book
And firmly ringed a word in one of your poems.
A ripple arrested —
'Death'.

Hugh Whitemore
London, 1983

ACT ONE

The cluttered sitting-room of a small semi-detached house in North London. Late afternoon.

There is a square bay-window with lace curtains, an upright piano covered with piles of books, a bureau and a mirror. Vases of dried rushes and honesty stand on tables alongside pot-plants and flowers. Antimacassars are draped over the well-worn chairs. There are a number of amateur watercolours and some framed sepia photographs hanging on the walls.

Upstage, Stevie's Aunt is watering the pot-plants. She is a form-idable old lady, with iron-grey hair standing upright in a fan-shaped frill. She is wearing a dress brightly patterned with flowers.

A MAN *enters and addresses the audience. He wears neutral, sombre clothes.*

MAN: Life is like a railway station, Stevie said. The train of birth brings us in, the train of death will carry us away. All aboard for a day in the suburbs.

[AUNT *continues to water the pot-plants.*]

STEVIE: [*off*] I'm back! [*She slams the front door.*] I'm back! Where are you?

AUNT: In here.

[STEVIE *enters, carrying a handbag and a plastic shop-ping bag. She is a small, hunched, bird-like woman, with a fringe of dark, straight hair. Her pale face has an expressive mobility, and her gestures are quick, with the spontaneity of a child. She is wearing a wine-coloured corduroy pinafore dress, with heavy-knit stockings and sandals. She kisses* AUNT.]

You're home nice and early.

STEVIE: I'm utterly exhausted, worn to a frazzle.

AUNT: The kettle's on, I'll make a pot of tea.

STEVIE: Is there anything to eat?

AUNT: Battenburg cake and some ginger nuts.

STEVIE: How lovely!

AUNT: Give me your coat.

STEVIE: Has anything happened today?

AUNT: Nothing out of the ordinary.

[AUNT *takes* STEVIE's *coat, and exits.*]

STEVIE: When I'm asked at the Day of Judgement what I remember best and what has ruled my whole life, I think I shall say: "Being tired, too tired for words." I've been at the BBC, recording a story. I don't know why I bothered, it was a complete waste of time. The producer seemed to have quite a different idea about the story from mine. We got more and more at cross purposes, and a Mr Hall, who was sitting on the floor listening, said he couldn't make head or tail of it.

[AUNT *enters, carrying a plate of cake and ginger nuts.*]

AUNT: Head or tail of what?

STEVIE: This is my aunt.

AUNT: Who are you talking about?

STEVIE: His name was Mr Hall.

AUNT: Head or tail of *what?*

STEVIE: A short story I'd written.

AUNT: Poor man, I know how he felt.

STEVIE: I call her the 'Lion of Hull'. She looks very lion-like, don't you think?

[AUNT *is searching amongst the books on the piano.*]

The dress is new, by the way. It reminds me of one of those seeds packets, you know, Carter's Tested Seeds. I call it 'Every One Came Up'.

AUNT: Where are my glasses, Peggy?

STEVIE: In the fruit bowl.

AUNT: All these books, just look at them!

STEVIE: Not a literary person, thank God.

AUNT: I've never seen so much stuff and nonsense in all my life.

[AUNT *exits.*]

STEVIE: Stuff and nonsense are the twin bogies of my dear Aunt's existence, and she tilts against these pet windmills with all the courage of a latter-day Don Quixote. 'Stuff and Nonsense' is her call to arms, her battle-cry.

[AUNT *enters, carrying the tea-tray.*]

AUNT: That stupid kitchen tap needs a new washer. Tarnation take it.

[*She goes to her chair.*]

Where's my cushion?

STEVIE: Here, sorry.

> [STEVIE *takes the cushion from the chaise and gives it to* AUNT.]

AUNT: You can never find anything in this house.

> [AUNT *pours the tea.*]

STEVIE: Smart writing people think it's not at all chic to live in the suburbs with an aunt, but I don't care what they think. I've never cared about chic things, fashion and so on. What does it matter? I love Aunt and Aunt loves me. That's what really matters.

AUNT: Tea, dear?

STEVIE: Thank you, darling.

> [STEVIE *takes a tea-cup from* AUNT, *who settles into her chair.* STEVIE *sits and sips tea.*]

AUNT: Good?

STEVIE: Mmm! Well now, where shall I begin?

AUNT: Begin at the beginning and go through to the end, that's what I always say.

STEVIE: Yes, and quite right too. Well. The twentieth of September, nineteen hundred and two: that was the beginning for me. The twentieth of September. Virgo. Rather a prim sign I always think, so I like to pretend I'm a bit of a Libra, too.

AUNT: A Yorkshire lass, born in Hull. Thirty-four Delapole Avenue, such a nice house.

STEVIE: We left when I was only three, so I don't remember much about it. Just wearing a pale blue coat, and having strawberries and cream on a vast stretch of bright green grass with people in white on it.

AUNT: A Cricket Club tea.

STEVIE: It must've been, yes. And so, on an autumn afternoon in nineteen hundred and six, my mother, my aunt, my five-year-old sister Molly and I arrived here in Palmers Green.

AUNT: All those years ago! It doesn't seem possible.

STEVIE: She was a romantic girl, my mama, and because of this she made what they call an 'unsuitable' marriage.

AUNT: If your grandma had lived, your mother and father would never have met, let alone married.

STEVIE: And where would Stevie have been then, poor thing?

AUNT: He was a great believer in independence, your grandfather. "Decide for yourself," he was always saying, and that's just what she did.

[*The front-door knocker bangs.*]

There's my paper.

[AUNT *exits.*]

STEVIE: My Mother was a romantic girl
So she had to marry a man with his hair in curl
Who subsequently became my unrespected papa,
But that was a long time ago now.

[AUNT *enters with the newspaper and sits reading.*]

What folly it is that daughters are always supposed to be
In love with papa. It wasn't the case with me.
I couldn't take to him at all
But he took to me
What a sad fate to befall
A child of three.

I sat upright in my baby carriage
And wished mama hadn't made such a foolish marriage.
I tried to hide it, but it showed in my eyes unfortunately
And a fortnight later papa ran away to sea.

He used to come home on leave
It was always the same
I could not grieve
But I think I am somewhat to blame

AUNT: Kent are doing badly: eighty-five for six.

STEVIE: So with my father sailing the seven seas, we came here to Avondale Road. When we had settled ourselves in, we went round the corner to our landlord's shop, he was a plumber, a tall, thin man who looked like Charles the Second, we went round the corner to make some arrangements and to get me weighed.

AUNT: You were always being weighed for one reason or another.

STEVIE: He had some enormous weighing machines, I remember, the sort they use for luggage.

AUNT: "You're a fine package," he said, lifting you onto the scales. "I came on a train," you said, "I came on a train, and then on a tram." And so you did, bless your heart.

STEVIE: He was wrong, that plumber. I wasn't a fine package at
         all. I was always being ill.

AUNT: That's why I came to London. Someone had to look after
         you, with your mother being so weak and poorly.

STEVIE: Yes, I often wish I'd been a bright, healthy child, but I
         wasn't and that's that. Fate, I suppose. Stevie's fate.

AUNT: Fate, indeed!

STEVIE: I believe in fate, I really do.

MAN: It's like a man playing cards, Stevie said. There's the man
         himself, and the cards he's playing, and there's another
         man watching over his shoulder. The player is life, the
         watcher is the spirit, and the cards are fate. Stevie's fate
         was unfortunate, to say the least. It was tuberculosis.

                    [STEVIE *lights a cigarette.*]

STEVIE: I spent months and months in a children's hospital, and
         actually thought of suicide for the first time when I was
         eight. The thought cheered me up wonderfully. "Life
         may be treacherous," I remember thinking to myself,
         "But you can always rely upon Death." It also occurred to
         me that if one can remove oneself from the world at any
         time, why particularly *now*? I realized that Death is my
         servant; he has got to come if I call him. I think every
         sensitive young child should learn this. It's a great source
         of strength and comfort.

AUNT: Love-nest vicar jailed for three years. Fancy that. Serve
         him right.

                    [*They laugh.*]

STEVIE: Eventually I got better, and came back home to Avondale
         Road.

         How sweet the birds of Avondale,
         Of Avondale, of Avondale,
         How sweet the birds of Avondale
         Do swoop and sing and call.

         My sister and I thought it a very beautiful house and a
         beautiful garden, and so it was, so it is. Although our
         cautious elders would at first only sign a lease for six
         months, we've lived here ever since. Mind you, it was a
         country place then, with woods going all the way up to
         Southgate Station, but I still find it very dreamy and

poetical. The people are charming too. They have a non-interfering helpful politeness, which is rather like old Chinese courtesy.

AUNT: Is it six o'clock yet?

STEVIE: Twenty to.

AUNT: Soon be time to do the vegetables.

> [STEVIE *glances at the vase of bulrushes that stands on the piano.*]

STEVIE: I picked those bulrushes when I was a girl. Molly and I found them in the dark, mysterious, wonderful woods where Trespassers were Forbidden. They've been here almost as long as I have. [*She smiles as memories flood into her mind.*] How well I remember it, how clearly! A ripe September time with the autumn sunshine in the air and the rich smell of acorns and damp mould and the Michaelmas daisies, especially there was the smell of the large Michaelmas daisies that grew in the churchyard. Of course it wasn't always September or always sunny, but that's how one is apt to remember past times, don't you think?

MAN: There never were so many poppies as there were then,
So much yellow corn, so many fine days,
Such sharp bright air, such seas.

STEVIE: This sunny time of a happy childhood seems now like a golden age; a time untouched by war, a dream of innocent quiet happenings, a dream in which people go quietly about their blameless business, bringing their garden marrows to the Harvest Festival, believing in peace, believing in progress — providing it was progress in the right direction — and believing in God. Believing also that the horrible things of life always happen abroad or to the undeserving poor, and that no good comes from brooding upon them. Oh yes, I was happy then. Very happy.

Mother, I love you so,
Said the child, I love you more than I know.
She laid her head on her mother's arm
And the love between them kept them warm.

> [AUNT *emerges from behind her newspaper.*]

AUNT: More tea, Peggy?

STEVIE: Yes, please.

[AUNT *refills the tea-cups.*]

Two old ladies lived next door to us in those days.

AUNT: Miss Jessie and Miss Emily.

STEVIE: Miss Jessie used to do a lot of work for missionary organizations and was always collecting clothes 'for the 'eathen'. She was a happy, cheerful person, unlike her sister, who was full of doom and disaster. It was from her, from Miss Emily, that we first learnt about the White Slave Traffic.

AUNT: Yes, your mother was very cross about it. "I've told you, Peggy," I remember your mother saying to you, "I've told you never to speak to strangers in the street or to take sweets from them. So run along and do as I tell you and don't worry your head about the White Slave Traffic."

STEVIE: But it was too late. Miss Emily had fired my imagination. "If a lady comes up to you," she said, "if a lady comes up to you in a closed cab and leans out of the window and asks you to get in, don't you have anything to do with her." Then she seized my hand, and pulled me close up to her. I can remember her old lady smell now: the lavender and the moth-balls, the dusty velvet ribbon and the menthol lozenges she used to suck and, sometimes, the faint smell of her old dog clinging about her skirt. "Don't you have anything to do with her," she'd say, "it's the White Slave Traffic." But what would happen if you yielded to the blandishments of this strange lady in a closed cab? Ah, that we did not know. I remember for a long time I used to think that the wax work child models displaying clothes in the draper's shop windows were really white slave children who had been changed into statues, and that here indeed might truly be discerned the sinister hand of the white slavers.

AUNT: I've never heard such nonsense.

STEVIE: Maybe not, but I believed every word of it.

AUNT: Stuff and nonsense. You should've known better.

STEVIE: I wasn't very old, was I? Seven or eight, at the most.

AUNT: Old enough to know better. You were at school, after all.

STEVIE: That's right, so I was. So I was. Schoolgirl Stevie. [*She laughs: a long, raucous chuckle.*] We had the most unusual

headmistress, I remember. [*She turns to her Aunt.*] What
was her name?

AUNT: What was whose name?

STEVIE: Our headmistress; tall woman, with glasses.

AUNT: I've no idea, quite forgotten.

STEVIE: Well, it doesn't matter. She was a Quaker lady, I
remember that; a Quaker lady with a real devotion for
teaching. She believed in discipline, and she had a high,
some people might think a rather simple, moral code,
and she used to recite her own moralistic verses at morning prayers:

I wish that I were some beautiful land
Called the Land of Beginning Again,
Where all our mistakes and all our heart-aches,
All of our poor foolish pain,
Could be dropped like a shabby coat at the door
And never put on again.
No, never more.

AUNT: Oh, that's rather good.

STEVIE: We didn't like that one very much. We thought it was
rather sloppy. But there was a fine touch of melodrama
about one of our headmistress's chief favourites, which
went something like this:

Tomorrow, she told her conscience,
Tomorrow I mean to be good,
Tomorrow I'll do as I ought,
Tomorrow I'll think as I should,
Tomorrow I'll conquer the passions
That keep me from heaven away;
But ever her conscience whispered
One word and one only: Today!

Tomorrow, tomorrow, tomorrow,
And thus through the years it went on;
Tomorrow, tomorrow, tomorrow,
Till youth like a shadow was gone,
Till age and her passions had written
The message of fate on her brow,
And forth from the shadows came Death
With the terrible syllable: NOW!

[STEVIE *laughs, rocking back and forth, with her hands covering her face.*]

Oh yes, we liked that one. Our headmistress, like other more professional readers of verse, didn't pull her punches when it was a matter of expression. That NOW! fairly shocked us all.

[AUNT *lowers her newspaper.*]

AUNT: There's a piece here about a man who owes the Income Tax people twenty-five thousand pounds. Twenty-five thousand! They were on to me fast enough last year. Twelve pounds short, and they were on to me fast enough. The devils!

[*She returns to her newspaper.*]

STEVIE: Like most of the class, I was devoted to our form mistress, a wonderful lady who combined geography with painting, and subsequently left us for ever to study Egyptology under Flinders Petrie. "Now, children," she'd say, "Have you got any large hat boxes or dress boxes at home?" Yes, yes our mamas had plenty of such boxes. "Then bring them along with you tomorrow, and bring some moss to lay in the bottom of the box and then we can begin our jungle scene." The next day we'd set to work in earnest, painting the insides of our box lids rich indigos and blues, ochres and greens until they looked to our inspired imaginations exactly like the jungles of a tropical forest. I've loved the tropics ever since—although I had and still have a horror of snakes.

MAN: Dearest Evelyn, I often think of you
Out with the guns in the jungle stew
Yesterday I hittapotamus
I put the measurements down for you
But they got lost in the fuss
It's not a good thing to drink out here
You know, I've practically given it up dear.
Tomorrow I am going alone a long way
Into the jungle. It is all grey
But green on top
Only sometimes when a tree has fallen
The sun comes down plop, it is quite appalling.
You never want to go in a jungle pool

In the hot sun, it would be the act of a fool
Because it's always full of anacondas, Evelyn, not looking
    ill-fed
I'll say. So no more now, from your loving husband,
    Wilfred.

> [AUNT *folds her newspaper and stands up. She picks
> up the tea tray.*]

AUNT: Beans or carrots, Peggy?

STEVIE: What are we having?

AUNT: Lamb.

STEVIE: Beans, then, please.

AUNT: Open the door will you, love. Beans it is.

> [AUNT *exits with the tray.*]

STEVIE: Actually, I was rather *mal vue* at school, and I'm sure with
reason, though I'd rather have been thought naughty
than stupid. I think perhaps I was too easily bored. Sometimes, even now, I indulge in the utmost limit of boredom, so that when the telephone rings it's like an Angel
of Grace breaking in on the orgy of boredom to which my
soul is committed. But by and large I'm a forward-look-
ing girl and don't stay where I am. "Left, right, be
bright", as I said in a poem. That's on the days when I'm
one big bounce, and have to go careful so as not to be a
nuisance. Above all, I try to avoid getting too despairing.
I try to remember what they said in the thirteen hun-
dreds: "Accidie poisons the soul stream."

MAN: Rapunzel Rapunzel let down your hair
It is I your beautiful lover who am here
And when I come up this time I will bring a rope ladder
    with me
And then we can both escape into the dark wood
    immediately.

STEVIE: Cool as a cucumber calm as a mill pond sound as a bell
Was Mary when she went to the Wishing Well.
She has not been seen since then
If you ask me she'll not be seen again.

MAN: I am a frog
I live under a spell
I live at the bottom
Of a green well.

I have been a frog now
For a hundred years
And in all this time
I have not shed many tears.

I am happy, I like the life,
Can swim for many a mile
— When I have hopped to the river —
And am for ever agile.

STEVIE: 'Twas the voice of the Wanderer, I heard her exclaim,
You have weaned me too soon, you must nurse me again,
She taps as she passes at each window pane,
Pray, does she not know that she taps in vain?

MAN: No man has seen her, this pitiful ghost,
And no woman either, but heard her at most,
Sighing and tapping and sighing again,
You have weaned me too soon, you must nurse me again.

STEVIE: Yes, there's a lot of sadness in these childhood poems, I'm afraid, but that's because one soon realizes how brief it all is: schooldays, summer holidays by the sea-side, those cloudless September afternoons. Sooner or later adult fears are bound to seep in. Heigh-ho, indeed they are. Sooner or later you're bound to realize that you're just another human being, nothing special, just an ordinary mortal like everyone else. What a terrifying moment that is.

MAN: You are only one of many
And of small account if any
You think about yourself too much.
This touched the child with a quick touch
And worked his mind to such a pitch
He threw his fellows in a ditch
This little child
That was so mild
Is grown too wild.

Murder in the first degree, cries Old Fury
Recording the verdict of the jury.
Now they are come to the execution tree.
The gallows stand wide. Ah, me, ah me.

Christ died for sinners, intoned the Prison
Chaplain from his miscellany.
Weeping bitterly the little child cries:
I die one of many.

STEVIE: I was still very young when my mother died. She had
suffered greatly. Poor dear mama, she made an unsuitable marriage, and no doubt my father found it
unsuitable too. Unsuitable marriages breed the Stevies of
this world, and a lot of other troubles as well.

[AUNT *enters, carrying a bowl of beans and a knife.*]

AUNT: The rat died, did I tell you?

STEVIE: What rat?

AUNT: The one who lived in the garden. He used to sit by the
fence, grinding his teeth. Big as a dog he was, I got quite
fond of him, poor old fellow. The dustmen heaved a
brick at him. "That's done for him," they said. And so it
had. Poor old fellow.

[*She begins to slice the beans.*]

STEVIE: Nineteen-eighteen.

AUNT: The end of the war.

STEVIE: Mother's heart attack.

AUNT: Ah, yes.

STEVIE: She'd had heart trouble for many years, and wasn't the
happiest of people, alas.

I have a happy nature,
But mother is always sad,
I enjoy every moment of my life,
Mother has been had.

Well, that's not entirely true. I often feel sea-sad myself,
loamishly sad, like Tennyson, with a sadness too deep for
words.

AUNT: Just like your poor mother, though she had every reason
to be sad. Your grandpa was a very impatient man, and
he had no patience with your mother, not a scrap; he

thought she was a peevish, dreamy child. Not that he was cruel, you mustn't think that, he was just thoughtless. He'd be unkind without meaning to be unkind. He'd laugh at your mother's fancies because he didn't understand them. I remember him laughing at the paintings she brought home from school.

STEVIE: I can't understand people who don't care for paintings. I can't understand them at all. My top favourite is in Venice, it's by Tintoretto, and it's called 'The Creation of the World'. It's a marvellous painting! There are lots of little animals streaming out of the hand of God. But one's turning back. He's had a look and decided to sit this one out. It's really marvellous!

AUNT: Your grandpa never understood such things, he tried to pretend they were a silly waste of time. He had no self-confidence, you see, that was the trouble; he was afraid to admit there were things he didn't understand. He used to say: "I have no strong feeling of confidence in myself. If I come into a room everybody will at once go out." And so he grew sadder and more impatient, and it was your mother who suffered most. Poor gentle creature, how she suffered.

STEVIE: One day when I came home from school, I saw she was having a heart attack. I gave her some medicine, there was nothing else I could do for her. She was very white in the face, and her lips were grey, and she couldn't breathe. And I was choked with fury and impotence, and choked with fears of helplessness and indignation. I raged against necessity, I raged against my very absent pa, I raged and fumed and spat. There was nothing else I could do.

[AUNT *sighs.*]

AUNT: "Off to Valparaiso, love daddy." That's all we ever heard from your father. Picture postcards with foreign stamps.

STEVIE: "Off to Valparaiso, love daddy." Yes. [*She lights a cigarette.*] When I grew too old for fairy tales, I started reading stories by minor Victorians with titles like *Mrs. Haliburton's Troubles* or *Lost Sir Massingberd.* How richly compostly loamishly sad were those Victorian days, with a sadness not nerve-irritating like we have today. How I love those damp Victorian troubles! The woods decay,

the woods decay and fall, the vapours weep their burth-
ens to the ground, man comes and tills the field and lies
beneath, and after many a summer dies the swan.

MAN: Wan
Swan
On the lake
Like a cake
Of soap.
Why is the swan
Wan
On the lake?
He has abandoned hope.

STEVIE: Yes, always someone dies, someone weeps, in tune with
the laurel dripping, and the tap dripping, and the spout
dripping into the water-butt, and the dim gas flickering
greenly in the damp conservatory. "Behind the laurel
bushes lay the corpse of Sir Vyvyan Markaby, baronet."
Eventually, of course, Providence tidies things up, yes,
and keeps the right people on the right side of calamity.
Providence always did that in Victorian books; Providence always tidied things up, and the heroines always
preserved a stiff upper lip, smiling to the end, when God
stepped in and made everything all right.

[AUNT *finishes slicing the beans, and stands up.*]

AUNT: Did you remember to get the sherry?

STEVIE: Yes, it's in my bag.

[AUNT *observes some crumbs on the floor by the coffee-
table.*]

AUNT: Just look at those crumbs. You wouldn't think I'd
hoovered up in here this afternoon.

[AUNT *exits.*]

STEVIE: The nurses said my mother died quickly in a minute. But
how long is that minute?

[*Brief pause. She takes a sherry bottle from her bag.*]

Did you hear about the death of the tigress Flo? She fell
backwards into her pool at Whipsnade, and lay there in a
fit. The pool was drained and Flo, that mighty and unhappy creature, was subjected to the indignity of artificial
respiration. Yes, they worked Flo's legs backwards and
forwards and sat on her chest. Sooner them than me,

you'll say, and sooner me than Flo, that couldn't understand and wasn't raised for these high jinks. Back came
Flo's fled spirit and set her on uncertain pads. She
looked, she lurched, and sensing some last, unnamable,
not wholly apprehended, final outrage, she fell, she
wimpered, clawed in vain, and died.

Tender only to one
Tender and true
The petals swing
To my fingering.

Is it you, or you, or you?
Tender only to one
I do not know his name
And the friends who fall
To the petals' call
May think my love to blame.

Tender only to one
This petal holds a clue
The face it shows
But too well knows
Who I am tender to.

Tender only to one
Last petal's latest breath
Cries out aloud
From the icy shroud
His name, his name is Death.

[STEVIE *turns, gazing at the silent* MAN.]

[*The* MAN *exits.*]

[STEVIE *pours sherry into two glasses.*]

Sherry!

AUNT: [*off*] What's that?

STEVIE: I've poured the sherry.

AUNT: [*off*] Just coming.

[STEVIE *sips her sherry and sighs pleasurably.*]

STEVIE: How lovely. Nothing nicer. Well, not much. [*She chuckles.*]
There was once a woman called Miss Hogmanimy, which
is certainly a name you'd want to get married out of. She

had a bright smile, a highly polished face and an un-provocative blouse. She was terribly wrought up over B-A-B-I-E-S and the way they're born, and she gave up her whole life to going round giving free lectures, complete with lantern slides, to young girls of school or school-leaving age. She had a special way of talking, I remember, like losing her puff in an uphill climb, a sort of breathless whisper.

[AUNT *enters.*]

AUNT: You're talking about that Miss What's-her-name.

STEVIE: Hogmanimy.

AUNT: Stupid woman. All that nonsense she used to talk.

STEVIE: Her heart was in the right place.

AUNT: Stuff and nonsense. Where's my sherry?

STEVIE: There.

AUNT: Thanks. I don't hold with such things. You should've stayed at home.

STEVIE: But of course I didn't. I went and sat in the school chapel with the other senior girls, eager to know exactly what happened.

AUNT: Yes, I can see it all: giggling and laughing and carrying-on.

STEVIE: Fourteen-year-old, why must you giggle and dote,
Fourteen-year-old, why are you such a goat?
I'm fourteen years old, that is the reason,
I giggle and dote in season.

AUNT: People like Miss Thingummy do more harm than good, if you ask me. [*She sips her sherry.*] What nice sherry!

STEVIE: Tio Pepe.

AUNT: Very nice.

STEVIE: To listen to Miss Hogmanimy you'd think that knowing how B-A-B-I-E-S are born was enough to solve all the problems of adolescence. There'd be no more coming out in spots and getting self-conscious about the senior prefect, nor getting a crush on the English mistress, nor feeling proud and miserable like you do at that time, before you get grown up. She was always going on about the beauty of the human body, but I can think of a good many things a lot more beautiful. She kept saying: Oh how beautiful it all is, and how it's the holiest thing on earth, and she'd pray a prayer first of all, and we waited and waited and hoped we'd get the facts, but no, it was all this funny breathless whisper. Being all tied up with love and religious sentiments, it was just impossible for her to get the medical side of the question across; she'd draw sections on the blackboard and stand her stout body in front of it, blushing furiously. The upshot of it was she wanted us to sign a paper saying that we'd never drink anything but ginger beer and cola and allied liquids.

AUNT: You'd have been better off playing hockey.

STEVIE: Poor woman, she tried hard but her wits were fuddled. I came away from the lecture with a profound aversion to the subject and a vaguely sick feeling when I heard of friends and relatives about to produce offspring. I used to pray for them and wash my hands of it, though at the same time I had plenty of deep down hopes that I wouldn't end up *intacta* like one of those depressed females that never get asked, never get the chance, and go around reeking with their unholy continence. As I grew older I guessed that copulation was probably first-class fun, but I'd no idea how one actually set about it, nor indeed how one ever managed to find oneself a suitable mate.

AUNT: Just like that girl in the paper.

STEVIE: What girl?

AUNT: Didn't I tell you? I'm sure I told you.

STEVIE: Not a word.

AUNT: Well, this girl wrote to the paper and said she'd seen a young man at the tennis club she'd joined so as not to feel lonely, and to get herself fixed up with a young man and a house or a flat and a baby. Anyway, this young man would do, she thought, he was all right. The question was how could she get him to propose — they hadn't actually spoken, you see — so how could she make him propose? Well, they published an answer and they said: "Arrange to play the last set with him and then linger hopefully and perhaps he will see you home."

STEVIE: Oh, what a wonderful phrase! "Linger hopefully"!

AUNT: "Linger hopefully and perhaps he will see you home."

STEVIE: I can just imagine it, can't you? Up and down the suburbs,
          up and down the provincial towns, up and down India,
          up and down Singapore and Shangai, there are girls who
          have arranged to play the last set and who are — linger-
          ing hopefully!

AUNT: Lingering hopefully!
          [*The both laugh.*]

STEVIE: Well, thank God those days are over. No more hopeful
          lingering for me.

AUNT: It wasn't all hopeful lingering, as I recall; there was quite
          a bit of sitting up in the bath, crying your eyes out over
          some boy or another.

STEVIE: That was Freddy, he comes later. Karl was first.

AUNT: Karl?

STEVIE: You remember Karl. He arrived on Christmas Day with a
          potted flower for you, and a two-volume translation of
          Faust for me.

AUNT: More books!

STEVIE: And a dreadful translation it was.

AUNT: Talking of Christmas reminds me of Miss Delabole. She
          was telling me that when the Dean of Westminstc. went
          into the Abbey for the early morning service one Christ-
          mas he saw only seven people were there. "Not enough,"
          he said, and went home. [*She finishes her sherry.*] I'll just go
          and look at the meat. Best end of neck. Feeling hungry,
          Peggy dear?

STEVIE: Yes, I am, rather.

AUNT: [*picking up a pot of geraniums*] Good girl. Dear-oh-dear,
          those geraniums aren't very happy. I'll give them a drink
          of water.

          [AUNT *exits, carrying the pot of geraniums.*]

          [*The clock chimes six.* STEVIE *lights a cigarette.*]

STEVIE: At the foot of the Duke of York's steps Karl said: "I love
          you, Stevie." It was December. There was snow on the
          ground. "I love you, Stevie." Oh my sweet Karl, how I can
          see you now, with all of sleeping, happily dreaming
          Germany in your blue eyes. A student of philosophy at
          the University of Berlin. *Ein Student der Philosophie.* Later
          we went into the country, we walked in the rain along a

country road. There was a dead vole sticking its paws upright, like a Christian.

Now Vole art dead
And done is all thy bleeding.

We walked up a path towards a forlorn-looking empty
house. Inside there was a musty smell reminiscent of
murder, suicide and avarice. We found some sacking and
lay down in each other's arms. "I love you, Stevie." He
loved me, but he didn't like the English. I loved him, but I
didn't like the Germans. "The Germans are neurotic," I
said, "and weak. Look at Berlin swarming with uniforms
and swastikas! They're cruel as well, with a vicious
cruelty, not battle cruelty, but a doing-people-to-death-
in-lavatories-cruelty. How evil is Germany today!" [*Brief
pause.*] And so we quarrelled. And so we parted.

                [AUNT *enters.*]

AUNT: It won't be long now.

STEVIE: Time for another sherry?

AUNT: Yes, please.

                [STEVIE *refills the sherry glasses.*]

You're smoking too much, Peggy. It's bad for you, bad
for your tubes.

STEVIE: The Lion Aunt always calls me Peggy, never Stevie.

AUNT: What's wrong with the name you were christened with,
I'd like to know.

STEVIE: Nothing's *wrong* with it.

AUNT: Well, then.

STEVIE: Stevie started as a joke, really. Someone saw me out
riding and thought I looked like Steve Donaghue, the
jockey, you know. Steve became Stevie, and it stuck.

AUNT: Peggy you were christened and Peggy you shall remain.
Where's the paper?

STEVIE: It's on the desk.

                [AUNT *takes the newspaper, and sits in her favourite
armchair.*]

When I left school I went to Mrs Hoster's famous
secretarial college, and then I got a job with Newnes, the
publishers. I've been there almost the whole of my so-
called, ha-ha, working life. All that capitalismus toil is

very difficult and exasperating indeed, but my
employers are kindly people and never complain about
my writing during office hours. Actually, I've grown
rather fond of my boss. He has a very dry sense of
humour. I remember once telling him about a newspaper article which said that there were three million
four hundred and thirty-two thousand five hundred and
twenty-one illegitimate children in the United Kingdom.
"Hoorah," he cried, "who says that England's going
pansy?"

> [AUNT *speaks without looking up from her newspaper.*]

AUNT: Say what you like, I always thought you'd marry Freddy.

> [STEVIE *turns, puzzled by this non-sequitur.*]

STEVIE: What?

AUNT: I can't think why you didn't.

STEVIE: What on earth are you talking about?

> [AUNT *lowers her newspaper.*]

AUNT: And don't try to shut me up. I wasn't the only one, after
all.

STEVIE: Not the only what?

AUNT: Person who thought you'd marry Freddy.

STEVIE: Marriage, marriage, always this talk of marriage!

AUNT: You made a fine old fuss when he went away.

STEVIE: That's not the point.

AUNT: What is, then?

STEVIE: I'm not the marrying kind, I never have been.

AUNT: You got engaged to him fast enough.

STEVIE: I shifted my mother's ring onto my engagement finger,
that's all. It was like a game, just a game.

AUNT: Nonsense.

STEVIE: I'm a friendship girl, not the marrying kind.

AUNT: Stuff and nonsense!

STEVIE: It's true! The very thought of marriage makes me
nervous, it frightens me.

AUNT: I've never heard such rubbish in all my life.

> [AUNT *loses interest in the argument and disappears
> behind her newspaper.*]

STEVIE: She doesn't understand, she never has, and it's pointless
trying to explain. I may look like a pocket Hercules, but
I'm dreadfully low in energy, and a tired person like me

just can't respond to love; either it's too much for her and
she'd rather be dead, or else she sees it as a desperate
chance clutch upon a hen-coop in mid-Atlantic. Oh, the
fights and ecstasies of the spirit and the sad pursuing
bones!

[*The* MAN *walks briskly into the sitting room.*]

MAN: Am I too early?

[AUNT *puts down her newspaper.*]

AUNT: Freddy, dear, how nice to see you! I thought you were
playing cricket.

MAN: Rained off. Damn shame; I was rarin' to go. [*He mimes an
off-drive.*] Biff! Straight through the covers!

AUNT: Come and sit down, dear. What a pleasant surprise!

MAN: How are you, Miss Spear? Keeping well?

AUNT: Oh yes, I mustn't grumble; well, I do, but I shouldn't, you
know how it is.

MAN: I do indeed, I do indeed.

AUNT: How are your parents?

MAN: Not too bad, all things considered. Dad's rheumatism's
been playing up a bit.

[AUNT *and the* MAN *continue their conversation in
dumbshow.*]

STEVIE: They always made me feel very welcome in Freddy's
house. Such kind, solid people. I was often invited to tea,
after a walk, say. And there's his kind mother. And
scones for tea. And they draw up to the fire and there's
talk about how awfully common the other people in
Palmers Green are being all the time. And how they have
their dinners in the kitchen and sit in their shirt-sleeves.
Suburbs people are always ashamed of being suburbs
people; they're always having to show that they're not like
that themselves, oh no, not like the others, oh no, not like
that.

MAN: They went up to town last week with the Westbrooks.
You know the Westbrooks?

AUNT: Yes, of course.

MAN: They saw the new Jack Buchanan show, very good, they
said. Dinner at the Troc afterwards, very jolly.

AUNT: The Westbrook girl's getting married, isn't she?

MAN: That's right, next month.

AUNT: Such a pretty girl. I can't think why she wasn't married years ago.

> [*She glares at* STEVIE.]

> [AUNT *and the* MAN *continue their conversation in dumbshow.*]

STEVIE: The people of Palmers Green have an idea, the un-married girls have an idea, that if only they were married it'd be all right, and the married women think: Well, now I am married, so it *is* all right. Sometimes of course it is all right, but sometimes they have to work very hard saying all the time: So now I'm married, so now it's all right, so Miss So-and-so isn't married, so that's not all right. And the girls who are not married are often getting quite desperate, oh yes, they're becoming quite desperate. They're saying all the time: If only I was married, if only I was married. It's like the refrain in 'The Three Sisters.' It's the *Leitmotiv* of all their lives. It is their Moscow.

MAN: They're having a bit of a do next Saturday, a cricket club do, you know, drinks and so on.

AUNT: Are you going?

MAN: We're both going.

STEVIE: Are we?

MAN: Well yes, I took it for granted.

STEVIE: You shouldn't take things for granted like that.

AUNT: Why on earth not? You're engaged, after all.

> [AUNT *and the* MAN *continue their conversation in dumbshow.*]

STEVIE: He'll have my heart, if not by gift his knife
Shall carve it out. He'll have my heart, my life.

> [AUNT *stands up.*]

AUNT: I'll just go and prod the joint. Mint sauce or redcurrant jelly?

STEVIE: I don't mind.

AUNT: I thought you preferred redcurrant; I bought some specially.

STEVIE: I really don't mind. You choose.

AUNT: You are a difficult girl sometimes.

> [AUNT *exits.*]

MAN: Pleased to see me?

STEVIE: Well, of course.

> [*The* MAN *takes an apple from the fruit bowl.*]

MAN: Pity about this damn rain; I felt like a knock this afternoon. Mmm, nice apples.

> [*He munches the apple, grins at* STEVIE, *then sits by her.*]

Give us a kiss and say you love me.

STEVIE: Not now.

MAN: She's in the kitchen, she can't see us.

STEVIE: Your mouth's full of apple.

> [*The* MAN *swallows hard.*]

MAN: All gone.

> [*The* MAN *moves to embrace* STEVIE.]

STEVIE: No, Freddy, please.

MAN: What's the matter?

STEVIE: Nothing's the matter.

MAN: You're in one of your moods.

STEVIE: I'm not in any sort of mood.

> [*Pause.*]

MAN: Is it because of, is it because of the other night? Is it?

> [*No response.*]

You agreed, you said yes. I didn't make you do it. Did I?

> [STEVIE *shakes her head.*]

What's wrong then?

STEVIE: Nothing.

MAN: Don't be daft, something's wrong. What is it? Don't sulk, tell me.

STEVIE: Why did you ask me if I was enjoying it?

MAN: What?

STEVIE: Right in the middle, you know, right in the middle of everything, you said: "Are you enjoying it?"

MAN: Did I?

STEVIE: "Are you enjoying it, dear?"

MAN: Well, sorry, I'm sorry. I didn't mean to offend.

STEVIE: Don't *say* that!

MAN: Don't say what?

STEVIE: I'm not *offended*!

MAN: What, then?

STEVIE: It's so typical, can't you see? It's so suburban.

MAN: Well, I am suburban. So are you.

> [*The* MAN *moves to embrace* STEVIE.]

Come on, Stevie, it's nothing to get upset about.

STEVIE: I'm not upset, I'm frightened.

MAN: Frightened of old Freddy?

STEVIE: Of getting married.

MAN: Don't be such a chump.

STEVIE: It's the truth. If I'm going to be a wife I want to be a good wife, and I don't feel up to being a good wife. It's my tubercular glands, I don't have the stamina.

MAN: That's just an excuse. [*Pause.*] Don't you love me any more?

STEVIE: Part of me does.

MAN: Well, thanks very much.

STEVIE: Of course I love you, you're strong and safe and comforting. It's just...

MAN: What?

STEVIE: If we get married, I won't be Stevie any more, I'll be Mrs Freddy. That's what frightens me.

MAN: It's the same for any other girl.

STEVIE: I'm not 'any other girl', I'm *me*. You take so much for granted!

MAN: Like what?

STEVIE: I don't know, everything. You expect me to behave in a certain way, to think in a certain way, to lead a certain sort of life. Well, I don't think I can do it. I don't think I want to.

[*The* MAN *is silent; he stands gazing at* STEVIE.]

I'm a friendship person, don't you see? The rhythm of friendship is strong in my blood: I must go, I must come back. Here I am again. Now I am going. I love people, but I love the thought and memory of them just as much. There comes a time when I have to go away, and then after a time, I must come back. It's a friendship rhythm, Freddy, I wasn't made for marriage. Don't you understand?

MAN: Not a word. I don't know what the hell you're talking about.

STEVIE: If only we could be friends.

MAN: Friends? What do you mean, *friends*? Grow up, Stevie!

STEVIE: Grow up?

MAN: Yes, grow up! You're like a child, living with your aunt, cossetted night and day, that's not a proper way of life for anyone. And don't start all that nose-in-the-air-arty-bohemian nonsense; you know it doesn't wash with me.

[STEVIE *and the* MAN *stare at each other.* STEVIE *turns away, bowing her head.*]

STEVIE: Oh, Freddy! How can we marry, how can we? It'd be utterly foolish, utterly suicidal!

MAN: You can't mean that.

STEVIE: Well, I do.

[*The* MAN *stands motionless, dumbstruck.*]

MAN: I see. Very well. If that's what you think.

STEVIE: Don't you? Honestly, don't you?

MAN: It could work. If you changed, it could work.

STEVIE: Why me? Why should I change?

MAN: You'll have to sooner or later, heavens above. Grown people don't spend their lives in a cocoon, writing poems with an old maid aunt.

STEVIE: I don't like change.

MAN: Then you'll be lonely.

STEVIE: All right, I'll be lonely.

MAN: You'll die alone, and you'll deserve to. Little pets like you deserve to be lonely.

STEVIE: Oh, go to hell.

MAN: Go to hell yourself.

STEVIE: Go to hell!

[*The* MAN *exits, slamming the front door.*]

[*Brief pause.*]

It's like escaping from a sunk submarine. You must stand quietly and without panic until the flood-water in the escape room is covering your shoulders, is creeping up to your mouth, and only then when the whole of your escape-room is flooded to drowning point will you be able to shoot up through the escape-funnel, to shoot up for ever and away. Then it's over. But when it's over, then it's tearing inside, it's 'tearing in the belly', and one wishes oneself dead and unborn. [*She lights a cigarette.*] When Freddy left, I ran a very hot bath and sat there, I just sat there in the water. And silently the tears fell down. I just sat there, my fringe all cock-awry, and the tears running down my cheeks into the hot water. It was as if the world had come to a sad, despairing, tearful end, but of course

it hadn't. One does little things and goes to see friends
and does one's work and fusses with this and that and
feels in one's heart the drift and dribble of penultimate
things. Kind friends tell you that Time is the only doctor,
and it's true. But he's a slow worker, that Time, and no
anaesthetist at all. Suddenly you have lost everything,
and the hours are long, and only a thousand hours will
help to heal.

Would he might come
Again and I
Upon his breast
Again might lie.

Would I had not
In foolish wrath
Driven him ever
From my path.

Would the sun
His day's course over
Might that same day's
Lost dawn recover.

As vain as this
Vain prayers are all
Vain prayers that would
Past days recall.

Never shall sun
Now sunk away
Rise up again
On yesterday.

Never shall love
Untimely slain
Rise from the grave
And live again.

And so one is left bitter, resentful and lonely, with this
sadness deficiency feeling. I tend to think that many
people carry this feeling around with them for most of
their lives. A lot of people pretend, out of bravery I
suppose, that they're very dull and ordinary chaps, but

really they don't feel at all at home in the world, and aren't able to make friends easily. Of course they joke a lot and laugh, and their chums think they're quite all right and jolly nice too, but sometimes they get tired and the brave pretence breaks down and then they are lost.

[*The* MAN *enters.*]

I wrote a poem about his once. I got the idea from a newspaper report about a man drowning.

MAN: Nobody heard him, the dead man,
But still he lay moaning:
I was much further out than you thought
And not waving but drowning.

Poor chap, he always loved larking
And now he's dead.
It must have been too cold for him his heart gave way,
They said.

Oh, no no no, it was too cold always
(Still the dead one lay moaning)
I was much too far out all my life
And not waving but drowning.

[*Silence.* STEVIE *sits motionless.*]

AUNT: [*off*] Peggy dear, dinner!

[STEVIE *does not move.*]

[*off*] Peggy!

STEVIE: Yes, coming.

AUNT: [*off*] Dinner's ready!

STEVIE: Coming!

[STEVIE *exits.*]

ACT TWO

Evening. The sitting-room is empty and dark.

STEVIE *enters. She is wearing her everyday outdoor coat over party clothes: a buttercup-yellow dress, silver lamé stockings and black patent-leather shoes with single straps. She switches on the lights.*

STEVIE: Dear-oh-dear. Parties! I do love them, but really, so tiring. By the time I've got myself ready, I'm totally exhausted and arrive looking like the sheeted dead. "Miss Stevie Smith," they call out, and in I walk: the sheeted dead.

AUNT: [*off*] Peggy!

STEVIE: Yes, it's me!

[STEVIE *takes off her coat.*]

And I never know what to do with my hands. I keep thinking: But *what* shall I do with my hands? Plus, of course, the ghastly problem of finding the bathroom. Whenever I get excited, I always dash straight for the bathroom. Nervous enteritis, they call it. Straight to the bathroom! It's so embarrassing, especially with strangers.

AUNT: [*off*] Peggy, is that you?

STEVIE: It's me, I'm back! [*She pours herself a brandy.*] The Lion Aunt's become a dreadful worrier, she worries about everything. She doesn't go out much either, well hardly at all. She thinks the house stood such a lot during the war that now it shouldn't be left. I know how she feels. It certainly stood an awful lot: the blitz, the doodlebugs, the V-2s. The Home Guard used to practise in the park, I remember, and there was a searchlight unit by the allotments. I became a fire-watcher, believe it or not, and used to patrol the streets near Trafalgar Square with my friend Norah Smallwood, who works for Chatto and Windus. Someone said that the middle classes were always the steadiest under fire. They didn't panic, you see, they were able to cope with the situation whatever it was. Well, I'm glad about that. I'm a middle-class girl myself, conditioned by middle-class thought, and it's nice

to know that we have our virtues. Heigh-ho, what a time it
was, the war I mean, my word yes. There were some
people called Rackstraw...

[AUNT *enters. She is wearing a plaid dressing gown.*]

AUNT: I've been calling and calling.

STEVIE: I thought you were just saying hello.

[AUNT *brandishes a buff-coloured envelope.*]

AUNT: Look at this. Another letter from those Income Tax
devils. You hid it in the fruit bowl.

STEVIE: Well, I don't suppose it's very important.

AUNT: It looks important. 'On Her Majesty's Service.'

STEVIE: What does it say?

AUNT: I haven't opened it.

STEVIE: Why not?

AUNT: I was waiting for you. What are you drinking?

STEVIE: Brandy. Do you want some?

AUNT: No, I'll have a cup of tea.

STEVIE: I'll get it, shall I?

AUNT: You stay here, I'll get it. How was the party?

STEVIE: Very jolly.

AUNT: Good.

[AUNT *exits.*]

STEVIE: Yes, she's getting old, becoming an old lady. [*She sighs,
and takes a sip of brandy.*] I must be careful not to give the
wrong impression. About being middle-class, I mean.
Suburbs people are extremely class-conscious, and I
don't approve of that, oh no. I was once in a terribly
refined tea shop in Evesham when a poor dirty old man
came in. He'd obviously made a mistake and didn't
realize how refined this tea shop was. The tea shop lady
was very snooty.

This Englishwoman is so refined
She has no bosom and no behind.

She took him gingerly by the coat-sleeve, and led him to
the door, she wouldn't have him there, no, no, it wouldn't
do at all. The old man went shuffling out, drips falling
down from his damp nose, and as he went out he said,
"It's a fooking stook-oop tea shop." Sometimes I think it's
a fooking stook-oop world, and quite often, I'm afraid,

it's the middle-classes who are the worst offenders. They're the ones who fight to the last ditch for the public schools and the privilege idea because they think they're so nearly about to clasp it, and so nearly about to send their kids to Eton. Never a thought for the kids, mind you, never a thought for the kiddos' welfare.

Parents who barely can afford it
Should not send their children to public schools ill will reward it.

[AUNT *enters with a glass of milk and a plate of game pie.*]

AUNT: I found a bit of game pie in the larder.

STEVIE: I thought you were going to have some tea.

AUNT: What?

STEVIE: You said you were going to make yourself a pot of tea.

AUNT: Did I? I changed my mind.

[AUNT *sits in the armchair, and takes out the Income Tax letter.*]

STEVIE: She keeps forgetting things.

AUNT: What?

STEVIE: Nothing.

AUNT: Look at it, Peggy, just look at it. "Do you make any repayment claims?" Well, do I?

STEVIE: Let me see. No, there's been some mistake. They think you are a man.

AUNT: A man?

STEVIE: They've called you Esquire.

AUNT: Disgraceful.

STEVIE: I shouldn't worry about it.

AUNT: If cousin James was alive I'd get him on to this.

STEVIE: Ignore it.

AUNT: He'd have known what to do.

STEVIE: Cousin James. He was one of the high-ups in Somerset House, very clever, very conscientious, and rather severe. He was a socialist of the Huxley-antimacassar period, when it was considered the acme of a man's right to work twelve hours a day, go to a night school free for another six, and then sleep for six hours on as hard a bed as could be found.

AUNT: He'd have sorted this out.

STEVIE: Yes, he probably would. He was always taking up legal cudgels on her behalf.

AUNT: Where's the writing-paper?

STEVIE: On the desk, but don't do it now. Do it in the morning.

AUNT: Never put off till tomorrow what you can do today.

> [AUNT *fetches her writing-paper.* STEVIE *lights a cigarette.*]

STEVIE: What was I going to say? Oh yes, the Rackstraws' dog. It was during the war and these people, the Rackstraws, they lived nearby, these people gave their dog to the Army to be trained for front line duties. But for some reason or another, maybe it was one dog too many for them, this dog was sent back home. After the training was complete, he was sent back home. I remember now, it was an injury to his right fore-paw, he was invalided out. The trouble was he'd been taught fierce ways, he'd been taught again his wolf behaviour, he'd been taught to fight and bite. So when his fond master went down the garden path to meet him, the dog leaped up, bared his fangs, and went to bite the throat of his loving friend. So the man clubbed him down with his heavy stick, so the dog died, and they buried him in the back garden. On his grave-stone they wrote: "He died for King and Country."

AUNT: How many Gs in aggravating?

STEVIE: Two.

AUNT: Two. Are you sure?

STEVIE: A-G-G-R-A-V. Two Gs.

AUNT: Well, you ought to know, it's your job after all.

STEVIE: [*rising*] The Lion Aunt has never approved of my writing. She doesn't disapprove either; she just thinks it's a waste of time, 'soppy' as she calls it, a soppy waste of time. Well, for years it was. I wasn't exactly a raging success in the thirties and forties, though I did manage to get my first novel published in nineteen thirty-six. I called it *Novel on Yellow Paper*.

AUNT: You do think up some daft titles.

STEVIE: I wrote it at the office, on the yellow paper we used for carbon copies.

AUNT: That doesn't make it any less daft.

STEVIE: Well, some people liked it, lots of people actually, people *and* critics. For a time I was almost a Name to Conjure With.

AUNT: Not for long, though.

STEVIE: No, not for long.

[*The* MAN *enters.*]

MAN: Sudden fame and then oblivion. That must have been hard to bear.

STEVIE: Hardly oblivion, my poems were still published. But you're right, it was hard; nobody likes being disregarded.

MAN: It's important to you is it, public recognition?

STEVIE: Of course; if you write something you want people to read it.

MAN: And that's why a writer writes: to be acclaimed, to be recognized?

STEVIE: Well, it's a reason, I suppose, not the reason.

MAN: What is the reason?

STEVIE: Oh I don't know, I couldn't say.

MAN: You must've thought about it, surely?

STEVIE: Not really, no I haven't. If you think too much about your inspiration you find that you're quite unable to write at all. It's like digging up flowers to see how they're getting on. "Where the apple reddens never pry."

MAN: I can't believe that a poem suddenly pops up and takes you by surprise.

STEVIE: Oh but they do, yes they do.

MAN: But there must be a reason why you start writing a particular poem. Is it personal experience, fantasy or what?

STEVIE: I write for myself really, to get something out that's working away at me. The pressures of life, you know, and fancies: the pressure of daily life, the pressure of having to earn one's living, the pressure of one's relations with other people, the pressure of despair.

MAN: What about happiness?

STEVIE: Well, it's not easy to get happiness into a poem, and often one doesn't want to. It spoils the fun. No, most of my poems get written from struggles and melancholy.

Happiness is silent, or speaks equivocally to friends,
Grief is explicit and her song never ends.

MAN: One hears a lot about the dreadful agonies of creation. Do you find writing a painful process?

STEVIE: Sometimes I do, sometimes I don't, it all depends. Of course there are those days when you think: I'm finished, I'll never write another word. Coleridge days, you know.

MAN: With the Person from Porlock knocking on the door.

STEVIE: Hammering's more like it. I do think he was a frightful cheat, don't you, Coleridge, blaming his bad days on some poor harmless visitor. I think he was already stuck in the middle of *Kubla Khan* and was just looking for an easy excuse.

> I long for the Person from Porlock
> To bring my thoughts to an end,
> I am becoming impatient to see him,
> I think of him as a friend.

It's difficult, you see — writing — it's a difficult business, difficult and exasperating. It can be very exasperating.

MAN: And painful?

STEVIE: Oh well, sometimes it is, but I don't mind. "Out of the tears the poems come", you know how it is.

AUNT: Yours faithfully. 'Yours faithfully' indeed! What nonsense putting that, you never mean it. Where are the envelopes?

STEVIE: Haven't they sent a label? They usually do.

AUNT: Oh yes, so they have.

MAN: You've published almost everything you've written. Do you ever regret this?

STEVIE: Why should I regret it?

MAN: Some of your work might seem to be a little unconsidered, a trifle hasty perhaps. Don't you wish you'd kept some of the poems until you could judge them more objectively?

STEVIE: When people hoard their poetry it usually means they're afraid, afraid of criticism. It's a weakness not a strength. When a poem's finished it's finished as far as I am concerned; it has its own existence and a right to see the light of day, which means that one must try to get it published. To do anything else is asking for trouble.

The monk sat in his den,
He took the mighty pen
And wrote "Of God and Men".

One day the thought struck him
It was not according to Catholic doctrine;
His blood ran dim.

He wrote till he was ninety years old
Then he shut the book with a clasp of gold
And buried it under the sheep fold.

He'd enjoyed it so much, he loved to plod
And he thought he'd a right to expect that God
Would rescue his book alive from the sod.

Of course it rotted in the snow and rain;
No-one will ever know now what he wrote of God and men.
For this the monk is to blame.

[AUNT *rises to her feet.*]

AUNT: I'm off to bed.

STEVIE: Sleep well, darling.

AUNT: [*kissing* STEVIE] And you, Peggy. God bless, happy dreams.
'Yours faithfully', indeed! Stuff and nonsense!

[AUNT *exits.*]

MAN: I wonder how you place yourself as a poet. Do you think of yourself as being typical, a typical example of a contemporary poet?

STEVIE: Typical? I don't know whether I'm typical, I don't know what that means. But then I'm alive today, therefore I'm as much a part of our time as everybody else; the times will just jolly well have to enlarge themselves to make room for me, won't they? And for everybody else. Being alive is being alive; being alive now is being alive now.

MAN: Yes, but you deliberately shun contemporary verse.

STEVIE: Do I? I wouldn't have thought so. Why do you say that?

MAN: You never read modern poets; nothing since Beowulf. Didn't you say that?

STEVIE: Only because I think it's dangerous. If you read too much, there's a danger you'll get your lines crossed and start writing other people's poems and not your own. It's not arrogance or anything like that; just self-preservation.

MAN: And what about your own poems, what effect do you think they have on the people who read them?

STEVIE: Oh I've no idea, none whatsoever.

MAN: None at all?

STEVIE: None at all! I often look at a poem and think to myself: I don't know why anybody reads any of it.

AUNT: [*off*] Peggy dear, I forgot the milk.

STEVIE: Yes, it's here.

AUNT: [*off*] Peggy!

STEVIE: Yes, I'll bring it!

[STEVIE *picks up the glass of milk and the pie.*]

I don't think these things matter very much, anyway; the whys and wherefores are beside the point. A poet should be made to get on with his writing and that's that, he should be put in a room with pencils and a pen or a typewriter, and be told to get on with it. And then if his poems are no good, he must be thrown out. A poet's not an important person; there'll always be another poet. [*calling upstairs*] Would you like a hot-water bottle?

AUNT: [*off*] Oh yes, please!

[STEVIE *exits.*]

[*Lights fade.*]

MAN: And so, for most of her life, Stevie followed her own advice and just got on with it: a part-time poet. Every morning she caught the Piccadilly Line tube to her office near the Strand, and every evening she travelled back to Palmers Green, to Avondale Road, and to the Lion Aunt. Life is like a railway station, Stevie said. One day they brought her home early, in great distress. Her wrists were bandaged.

She took her knife
Its cruel edge would bite
Into her flesh
Had she the resolution or the art
To bear the smart
And drive it to her heart?

Death, that sweet and gentle friend, failed to respond to
her summons. Life continued.

[*The* MAN *exits.*]

[*Lights come up to day.*]

[AUNT *enters with a blanket. She sits in the armchair
and drops the blanket on the floor.*]

AUNT: Peggy! Peggy!

STEVIE: [*off*] Just coming!

[AUNT *tries to pick up the blanket.*]

AUNT: Tarnation take it! Peggy, what are you doing? Peggy!

[STEVIE *enters, wheeling a trolley of food. She is wearing a blouse, tweed skirt, ankle socks and sandals.*]

STEVIE: Here you are: a nice ham salad.

AUNT: My soppy blanket's on the floor.

STEVIE: So I see. Come on, let's tuck you up.

[STEVIE *rearranges the blanket.*]

There's a special treat for pudding.

AUNT: What?

STEVIE: Eat your salad first.

AUNT: What is it, Peggy?

STEVIE: A special treat. Eat your salad.

[AUNT *begins to eat.*]

She can't do much these days, poor darling, and it's up to
me to run the house. She abdicated with great reluctance,
as you can imagine. Now that I'm leading a domestic sort
of life, I'd rather do the washing-up than write. Housework's the most wonderful excuse for not doing anything
else. I mean, clearing up a room, throwing everything
away, it's marvellous. Then you're tired out, so you go to
sleep all the afternoon. I love going out and getting the
food and chopping it up, hacking it up. It's a wonderful
way of getting rid of aggression! When I write, I write in
the back room after tea. It's a nice room, with a good view
of the garden and the birds.

[*She turns to* AUNT.]

Is everything all right?

AUNT: Lovely, dear, thank you.

STEVIE: Dearest Lion Aunt.

I will never leave you darling
To be eaten by the starling
For I love you more than ever
In the wet and stormy weather.

AUNT: Tasty ham.

STEVIE: It's York.

AUNT: Yes, I thought so. Very tasty.

STEVIE: Junket's her top favourite. Stevie's special junket. When it's set, I grate nutmeg all over it and then add a tablespoon of brandy or whisky. It's really delicious.

It was a house of female habitation,
Two ladies fair inhabited the house,
And they were brave. For although Fear knocked loud
Upon the door, and said he must come in,
They did not let him in.

And so we pass our days: housework, cooking, writing and the occasional glass of sherry. I've retired now of course, I retired early, and it's simply marvellous not having to go into the office every day. I wasn't cut out for the business world, I just didn't fit in.

[*She opens the window.*]

Lunchtime! Lovely bacon rind! Meal-o!

[*She throws the bacon rind into the garden and closes the window.*]

No, I never fitted in, like the little boy in the commercial class who was told to try his hand at commercial correspondence. "Dear Sir," he wrote, "Sadly we see our customers falling away from us, but I hope that we shall always be friends. And so, with love." They soon taught him business language, oh yes, he was soon corrected. But not me, not Stevie, I was always slightly out of step. I used to think I should've been a pirate or something, a North Sea pirate. We're all seafaring men in our family, after all, even my poor father. It was good for me, though, the office routine, I needed the discipline. If I'd never had to work I'd have become some sort of invalidish person and never done any writing; it was exile from domesticity that produced my poems. I enjoyed a lot of it too, office life, oh yes. I loved the stock exchange language they used, with its curious religious undertones: conversion, redemption, pegged at sixty. Marvellous! It wasn't a taxing job either, far from it. I used to sit in my tiny office, writing poems and books, and asking my friends round for tea and hot buttered toast. My boss never complained, never, never so much as gave me a reproachful glance, he was very kind. [*She chuckles.*] He used to advise me about stocks and shares. "Have you anything in Gossards?" he'd say. "If you've anything in Gossards, then sell." My word, how we laughed. Dear Sir Frank, I can see him now: walking past my office door in dark, dark mourning clothes and a dark, dark top hat. He was forever going to funerals. "Another good man buried," he'd say, and walk on with sombre tread.

[*Brief pause. She rises. The smile fades from her face.*] There's not much to say about the suicide business; it's something I'd rather forget. It's too painful, too much remorse. Not because of the act itself, no, one regrets the pain one inflicts on other people. Aunt. Sir Frank. My friends at the office. It shouldn't have happened there, not like that, poor Sir Frank was dreadfully upset. Upset, but not surprised, I doubt very much whether he was greatly surprised. "I'm rather disturbed about this death feeling in your poems, Stevie," he said to me once. He knew. Oh yes, he knew.

[*She is silent for a moment; her head bows forward.*]

AUNT: I've finished. Peggy, I've finished.

STEVIE: What?

AUNT: It's all gone, every mouthful.

STEVIE: Good, that's splendid. Now for pudding.

[*She brings the bowl of junket and the cream to* AUNT.]

Here you are.

AUNT: Junket! What a treat!

[STEVIE *pours cream over the junket.*]

STEVIE: And some cream to go with it.

AUNT: How kind of you, Peggy. Oh, you have been a busy girl.

[STEVIE *lights a cigarette; when she speaks her tone of voice is bright and animated, with no hint of suicidal despair.*]

STEVIE: Oh yes, I seem to be tremendously busy these days. I've got a lot of darling friends and I get entertained pretty freely, always dashing off to brasserie, bar, club and pub. Every so often, when Aunt's feeling well enough to cope by herself, I go week-ending in the country. I love it when people ask me back: "Do come again, Stevie." I think they're the best words of all. "Do come again."

> [STEVIE *chuckles.*]

AUNT: This is delicious, Peggy.

STEVIE: Good.

AUNT: What a treat!

> [AUNT *continues eating.* STEVIE *watches her with warm affection.*]

STEVIE: It was a little captive cat
Upon a crowded train
His mistress takes him from his box
To ease his fretful pain.

She holds him tight upon her knee
The graceful animal
And all the people look at him
He is so beautiful.

But oh he pricks and oh he prods
And turns upon her knee
Then lifteth up his innocent voice
In plaintive melody.

He lifteth up his innocent voice
He lifteth up, he singeth
And all the people warm themselves
In the love his beauty bringeth.

Some critics get awfully cross when I write cat poems, they seem to think it's letting the side down somehow.

AUNT: Is there any more, Peggy?

STEVIE: I think you've had enough, don't you?

AUNT: Just another spoonful, it can't do me any harm.

STEVIE: All right, then, just one.

> [STEVIE *serves a second helping of junket.*]

Don't eat too fast and give yourself heart-burn.

AUNT: Thank you very much. What a lovely lunch!

STEVIE: Lovely lunches follow lovely breakfasts and at night it's "God Bless, happy dreams." Nothing changes. Heigh-ho! The other day I came across a copy of *King Solomon's Mines*, which I'd been given as a Sunday School prize, and on the paper cover at the back of the book I could still read my childish handwriting: Florence Margaret Smith, One Avondale Road, Palmers Green, North London, England, North-West Europe...

STEVIE: ⎫
AUNT: ⎬ [*together*] The World!

STEVIE: Well, I'm still here and so is Palmers Green, though it's now very large and bustling, and in a social sense I suppose it's gone down. But really it's the same high-lying suburb it ever was. The top of our hill is the highest spot between here and the Ural mountains, or so they say.

AUNT: And so it is.

STEVIE: So it is.

AUNT: It is.

STEVIE: And it's still a very active place: we've got our Art Circle, Shakespeare Reading Society, Players' Guild, the Library Discussion Group, tennis clubs, croquet clubs, swimming clubs, riding clubs, and branches of the Labour Party, the Liberal Party, the Communist Party and the Primrose League. We also have our fair share of intellectual revolutionaries. These people see the middle-classes as obstructionist box-dwellers whose only thought is for themselves and their families — as if that were not the common thought of the greater part of mankind. They're the salt of the earth, these free-blowing revolutionaries, but it's wise to remember that you can't make a diet of salt alone.

> [STEVIE *wheels the trolley off, singing a familiar hymn-tune to herself. She returns to see that* AUNT *is beginning to doze.*]

Of course life has changed, and there are many things I miss: the lantern lectures in the Parish Hall, the dark mysterious wonderful woods where Trespassers were Forbidden — and which is now a housing estate — and those brightly-painted advertisements that used to

decorate the blank brick walls of our Swiss-chalet railway
station: "The Pickwick, the Owl and the Waverley Pen,
they come as a boon and a blessing to men." And there
was a striking poster for Jeyes' Fluid, I remember: a
nurse — with something, one feels, of Lady Macbeth in
her character — was slowly washing her hands, with her
eyes staring straight ahead. She knows that Jeyes' Fluid
can never wash out that stain, but it might perhaps dis-
infect it.

> [*A soft snore from* AUNT *makes* STEVIE *look round.*
> AUNT*'s head is lolling forward, and she is fast asleep.*]

She used to be such a brisk, managing person, and now
she sleeps her life away.

> [STEVIE *strokes* AUNT*'s cheek.*]

There is little laughter where you are going, and no
warmth. In that landscape of harsh winter, where the
rivers are frozen fast and the only sound is the crash of
winter tree-branches beneath the weight of the snow that
is piled on them — for the birds that might have been
singing froze long ago, dropping like stone from the cold
sky — there the soul is delivered to a slow death. [*Brief
pause.*] I don't mind much about survival, I mean, sup-
posing we had to go on for ever, how awful! Without
death, I don't think one could possibly endure life. It's an
escape from pain, of course, but also an escape from
pleasure too prolonged. It's rather like being drawn into
a race of water before it gets to the waterfall, it gets
quicker and quicker and more exciting; as you grow
older the more exciting it becomes. I don't know why
people are taught that Death is such a calamity, I think he
must rather be a dish. Besides, we all have to go some time.

> [AUNT *wakens, and looks around sleepily.*]

AUNT: Soon be time for a glass of sherry.

> [AUNT *removes her spectacles, and rubs her tired eyes.*
> STEVIE *takes the spectacles.* AUNT *sleeps. Pause.*]

STEVIE: I think of myself as an Anglican agnostic, if such a thing is
possible. I was brought up an Anglican, and I still like it
very much — I love the hymns! — I just don't believe it
any more. I reject the comfort and sweetness of Christianity because I feel that it's not true. And it's cruel, too,
hideously cruel.

Is it not interesting to see
How the Christians continually
Try to separate themselves in vain
From the doctrine of eternal pain.

They cannot do it
They are committed to it,
Their Lord said it,
They must believe it.

So the vulnerable body is stretched without pity
On flames for ever. Is this not pretty?

The religion of Christianity
Is mixed of sweetness and cruelty
Reject this Sweetness, for she wears
A smoky dress out of hell fires.

Who makes a God? Who shows him thus?
It is the Christian religion does
Oh, oh, have none of it,
Blow it away, have done with it.

This god the Christians show
Out with him, out with him, let him go.

I suppose it's because we're so lonely, because Man is so
lonely, that we must invent God. I think one should just
accept loneliness, not make a theology out of it. If I'd
been the Virgin Mary, I'd have said: "No, no, I'll have no
part in it, no saviour, no world to come, nothing." [*Brief
pause.*] People think because I never married I know
nothing about the emotions. They are wrong. I loved my
Aunt.

> [STEVIE *leads* AUNT *off.*]

> [*Lights fade, then come up to full.*]

> [*The* MAN *enters, assuming the persona of an urbane,
> slightly mannered literary-fringe figure.*]

MAN: I first met Stevie shortly after the war. Well, I say shortly,
but in fact it was a little longer than that. A little longer
than shortly. It must've been at one of those noisy quasi-
bohemian gatherings to celebrate somebody's book or
somebody's exhibition or somebody's first night or some-

body's something. All the familiar faces were there: Johnny Minton, Colquhoun and Macbryde, Tambi- muttu, Maclaren-Ross. I was wondering how much longer I could put up with all that shrill chatter and cigarette smoke when I saw a strange-looking creature hiding in a corner and drinking gin with considerable verve. I went across and introduced myself. She gave me what can only be described as a radiant smile, and told me her name was Stevie Smith. I knew her work of course, and admired its quirky individuality. We had one of those brief shouted cocktail-party conversations, mostly about the row Stevie was having with George Orwell, who had been her producer at the BBC. "He keeps lying to me," she said, "I'm bored to death by the lies."

STEVIE: [*off*] Help yourself!
MAN: What?
STEVIE: [*off*] Help yourself to a drink.
MAN: Thank you dear. [*He pours himself a gin and lime.*] After a while, she asked me if I'd give her a lift to Palmers Green; it seemed rather a long way away, but I was grateful for the chance to escape. I soon learnt that she always expected her car-owning friends to ferry her about, no matter how inconvenient it might be. God knows how many trips I've made on her behalf through the beggarly purlieus of north London! These rather tiresome duties have now reached a peak with Stevie becoming some- thing of a star turn on the poetry reading circuit, which means a lot of travelling for Stevie and a certain amount of nervous exhaustion for her car-driving friends. Even so, my affection for her has survived, relatively un- impaired.

       [STEVIE *enters, struggling to put on a tweed jacket.*]
STEVIE: Why, in a crisis, are one's coat-sleeves always inside out?
MAN: Let me help.
STEVIE: No, no, I can manage.

       [STEVIE *parades in front of the* MAN, *displaying a badly dyed green dress.*]
       How do I look?
MAN: Very nice.
STEVIE: That means you hate it.

MAN: Not at all. It's very striking.

STEVIE: I dyed it myself.

MAN: So I see.

STEVIE: 'Caribbean Blue' it said on the packet, but it looks more greenish to me. What do you think?

MAN: Well, it's a bit patchy, Stevie, just a bit uneven.

STEVIE: [*searching for something amongst the debris on the piano*] Oh that doesn't matter, they'll think it's a part of the pattern or something.

    With my looks I am bound to look simple or fast
      I would rather look simple

    Anyway it's warm, that's the main thing. Those school halls are always so draughty.

MAN: You should've worn trousers.

STEVIE: Not me, darling, never trousers. Never trousers on principle. [*She chuckles.*] Did I tell you about that?

MAN: Tell me about what?

STEVIE: This Colonel I met at a hotel somewhere, Colonel Peck I think his name was, I could've hugged him. There was this lady, you see, this large English lady who always wore trousers. She wore them on principle, she told us at breakfast one morning. And a pretty fat principle too, said the Colonel. I could've hugged him!

        [*She finds what she is looking for, a brooch in a tin box.*]

    Ah, here it is. I knew I left it somewhere on the piano. [*glancing in a mirror*] Dear me, what a sight. I look a bit below par, don't I? A couple of sherries below par. Just like that ghastly photograph.

MAN: What ghastly photograph?

STEVIE: The one I showed you last week, the one that made me look as if I'd been dead for a very long time. I don't mind looking old, but I do have a thing about looking dead and buried. [*turning to the* MAN] Brooch or necklace, which do you prefer?

MAN: Either, Stevie, you look charming in either.

STEVIE: Don't be so boring. Tell me what you think.

MAN: I think we ought to hurry up. It's time we were going.

STEVIE: Not yet, surely?

MAN: It's gone half past.

STEVIE: It won't take us more than a couple of hours.

MAN: We ought to allow three.

STEVIE: Two hours maximum, they said on the tephelone. [*sic*]

MAN: The traffic gets bad at this time of day.

STEVIE: Well, we can't go yet, I haven't packed a bag.

MAN: What bag? You don't need a bag.

STEVIE: I thought I'd take an overnight bag.

MAN: What on earth for?

STEVIE: Just to be on the safe side, you never know.

MAN: But we're driving straight back. That's why I'm here! We're driving straight back after the reading.

STEVIE: You never know, darling, somebody might ask us to stay.

MAN: Who? Who?

STEVIE: People do sometimes, it's possible.

MAN: I've got a meeting first thing in the morning.

STEVIE: [*picking up her coat*] All right, come back, I'm not stopping you.

MAN: Meaning you'll stay?

STEVIE: Well, of course, if I'm asked. It'd be fun to have a party. It's so dull in London, don't you think, one never meets other writers, it's not like France, is it? Poets and writers don't go and sit in pavement cafés, it's not like Paris. Well, the pavements are so awfully cold. And you can't just go up to people and say: "You're a poet and so am I, so I'm coming to dinner next Thursday."

MAN: Stevie, this is ridiculous.

STEVIE: What is?

MAN: If you're staying overnight, you could've caught a train.

STEVIE: I didn't say I *was* staying. I just said I'd like to.

MAN: It's a bloody awful drive.

STEVIE: You said it wasn't.

MAN: A hundred miles there, a hundred miles back.

STEVIE: Well, you offered.

MAN: You asked.

STEVIE: You could've said no.

MAN: Look, I'm driving up because there's no train back tonight...

STEVIE: Yes and I'm very grateful, I told you I was grateful, I don't know what more I can say.

MAN: Then why all this talk of staying overnight?

STEVIE: I only mentioned it as a possibility.

MAN: You should've told me before.

STEVIE: I won't ask you again, don't worry. Never again, never, never, nevermore. Quoth the Raven.

[*She pours herself a gin.*]

MAN: What are you doing now?

STEVIE: Having a drink, what does it look like? [*She sips her gin.*] It's not very kind of you, carrying on like this. How was I to know you'd want to get back straight away? I didn't know you went to meetings and things. It's very upsetting.

MAN: All right, I'm sorry. [*He goes to* STEVIE.] I'm sorry. Let's stop this bickering, shall we?

STEVIE: I'm not bickering.

MAN: Let's get a move on, then, otherwise we won't get there at all.

STEVIE: Well, I'm ready. I was ready ten minutes ago.

MAN: I thought you wanted to pack a bag?

STEVIE: There's no point, is there, if we're driving straight back. [*She goes to the door.*] I'll just get the food.

MAN: What food?

STEVIE: I bought some sausage rolls; I thought we'd need a snack on the way. We'll take some glasses, too. Have a drop of gin.

[STEVIE *exits.*]

MAN: Dear, darling Stevie. She needed to be cherished, she needed to be lapped in loving care.

In the midst of *so* much love
And such comfort
Still to feel unsafe and be afraid,
How one's heart goes out to you!

I remember once sitting at the back of a cheerless school hall while Stevie pranced about on the stage, chanting her poems like an elderly Shirley Temple. It should've been embarrassing, but it wasn't; it was touching, truthful and haunting, and the schoolchildren were enthralled. She spoke to them directly, you see: from child to child, from heart to heart.

STEVIE: [*off*] I thought you were in a hurry!

MAN: Coming, Stevie.

STEVIE: [*off*] Don't forget the gin.

> [*The* MAN *picks up the gin and exits.*]

> [*Lights fade.*]

> [*Lights come up to day. The sitting-room is empty. The clock chimes.*]

> [STEVIE *enters with a new coat, a new hat, a new silk scarf, two handbags, and a new pair of gloves. She is limping slightly. She puts the new clothes on the armchair.*]

STEVIE: I've got a bad leg. What a bore.

> [*She begins transferring the contents of her old handbag into the new one.*]

It was quite awful, I had to do a broadcast for the BBC and I told them about the leg, quite casually, you know. Well, they sent a car for me *and* a rug. All I needed was a shawl and a hot-water bottle to complete the picture! Everything has its compensations, I suppose, even getting old. Of course, I miss Aunt dreadfully. When you live with an old lady from an early age you never cease to be a child. Now she's gone and I find I'm old myself. Some people thought I should move: "Why don't you get a flat in London?" they said, but I didn't want to, I didn't want to leave Avondale Road. Everybody's so kind to me here, I'm better off in Palmers Green, and I've got used to living alone, oh yes, I quite like it. It's wonderfully dreamy to be in a house all by yourself; you can wander around and sleep in a different room every night if you want to. And if I'm tired, I just stay in bed. It's extraordinary how unaware one is of time passing. Some days are long and thin and there is nothing in them, but they speed past just the same. And suddenly you realize how short it all is, life, and how at the end comes death with the pleasure of certainty. I read a lot these days, I read more than ever, Gibbon especially. *Decline and Fall* is my favourite book, I never tire of it. I like Agatha Christie, too. I love reading her stories in French, it makes it all so wonderfully funny: "*Je suis un détective. Je m'appelle Hercule Poirot.*" I think she's a genius. "*Preparez vous à reçevoir un choc: votre patron, Mr Rachett, est mort!*" Her murders are so polite.

[*She starts putting on her new coat and hat.*]

Oddly enough, life has suddenly become rather exciting, and I'm now quite a celebrity. I've been photographed for the papers, I've been interviewed for the television, I've made gramophone records, I've lectured, I've even had my portrait painted. Mind you, it wasn't much like me, I didn't think so anyway. The colouring was lovely, but the lower part of the face seemed to belong to somebody else. To Disraeli, I think.

[*She sings:*]

Do take Muriel out
She is looking so glum
Do take Muriel out
All her friends have gone.

All her friends are gone
And she is alone
And she looks for them where they have never been
And her peace is flown.

Do take Muriel out
Although your name is Death
She will not complain
When you dance her over the blasted heath.

[*She picks up the new handbag.*]

The most exciting thing of all was getting the Queen's Gold Medal for Poetry. This was a tremendous honour and I was tremendously pleased about it and very flattered too. It used to be sent by post, I believe, but Cecil changed all that when he became Poet Laureate, and quite right too. Just imagine getting a gold medal from the Queen with all those gas bills and postcards from Felixstowe! "Anything in the post today, dear?" "Oh, just a gold medal from the Queen." Anyway, they told me to get to Buckingham Palace at such-and-such a time, and of course I was terrified of being late. I'm always late for everything. I had a fortifying drink at the Ritz and then walked through the rain to the Palace. I got there desperately early and they were still in the middle of Changing the Guard, so what to do? The only thing I could think of was to go next door to the Queen's Gallery, where I bought a whole lot of postcards, da Vinci drawings, which I had to cram into my handbag, it's not very big as you can see. So there I was, with a handbag full of postcards, standing in the rain outside Buckingham Palace. I walked up to one of the policemen and said, "I'm supposed to be in there, you know, I've got an appointment with Her Majesty to have this medal." To my surprise, he knew all about it and in I went, into the Palace. I was met by a rather decorative young man in naval uniform, and he took me into an outer room, whatever it's called, a huge room, and there was this lady-in-waiting, a most agreeable girl, and we had a very giggly time. She asked me to do a poem, so I hissed a short one under my breath, the one about a poor débutante sitting alone at a grand ball. It seemed appropriate, I thought.

I cannot imagine anything nicer
Than to be struck by lightning and killed suddenly crossing a field
As if somebody cared.
Nobody cares whether I am alive or dead.

My word, yes, we had a very jolly time. I adored that part of it. Then the One Before Me came out: a staggering-looking woman. Heavens, I thought, I'm not properly dressed for this — I found this hat in a jumble sale, only five shillings, a tremendous bargain, but perhaps a bit of a mistake. Anyway, the young naval man took me to the door, and there far, far away — the room's as big as Trafalgar Square — standing against the mantelpiece, was this charming figure, the Queen. I'd never seen Royalty close to before, well only once before. I saw the Queen Mother at the Book Prints Exhibition. I was standing on the first floor landing, and she walked below me. I could've poured sherry on to her hat. So there she was, there was the Queen. You curtsy and make your way across the room; then she comes forward and smiles, she's got a very gracious smile, and gives you the medal.

As she gave it to me she said, "I don't know what you'll do with it." I looked at it and said, "Well, I suppose I could have a hook put on it and wear it round my neck." "I don't know whether it's real," she said. "Oh," I said, "I'm sure it is." Then she motioned me, I think that's the expression, she motioned me to sit down. There was a table between us. They'd told me outside not to worry about when to come out because she'd ring a bell under the table. Well, the poor darling kept on asking me questions about poetry, and I got the impression it wasn't exactly her favourite subject. "How do you think of a poem?" she asked. "Well," I said, "it just sort of comes to you, often when you least expect it. Right in the middle of hoovering, you know, you suddenly think of a poem." She made me feel awfully like a schoolgirl again, being interviewed by a rather cordial headmistress. After a while I got a bit nervous and said, "I don't know why, but I seem to have written a lot about murder lately." This was obviously the wrong thing to say; the royal smile got rather fixed. When it's all over you walk out backwards, curtsy at the door, and the young naval man gets a taxi for you. We went to the Epicure afterwards for a celebration lunch: Cecil Day Lewis, Eric Walter White — from the Arts Council — and Norah Smallwood, my fire-watching chum from Chatto's. Dear Eric ordered oysters, which was a great mistake; they took ages to arrive, and I had to ask the waiter for some bread and jam to stave off the pangs. Then back to Avondale Road. [*She is silent for a moment, smiling at the memory.*] I so wished that the Lion Aunt could've been alive to see it. Perhaps she'd have changed her mind about my writing. Perhaps not. Stuff and nonsense! Perhaps she was right, heigh-ho.

> [STEVIE *chuckles. She stands motionless, a frail figure in her best clothes, with the jumble-sale hat pulled down over her fringe of hair.*]

> [*The* MAN *enters.*]

> [STEVIE *sits in the armchair.*]

I have a friend
At the end
Of the world.
His name is a breath

Of fresh air
He is dressed in
Grey chiffon. At least
I think it is chiffon.
It has a
Peculiar look, like smoke.

It wraps him round
It blows out of place
It conceals him
I have not seen his face.

But I have seen his eyes, they are
As pretty and bright
As raindrops on black twigs
In March, and heard him say:

I am a breath
Of fresh air for you, a change
By and by.

Black March I call him
Because of his eyes
Being like March raindrops
On black twigs.

But this new friend
Whatever new names I give him
Is an old friend. He says:

Whatever names you give me
I am
A breath of fresh air,
A change for you.

> [*Pause.*]

MAN: Stevie's sister Molly suffered a severe stroke, which left her virtually helpless. Anxious to do what she could, Stevie packed her bags, said good-bye to Avondale Road and went to Devon, to Buckfastleigh, where Molly lived. It was there that she became ill. From Torbay Hospital she wrote to an old friend.

STEVIE: Dear John, I am ill now which means I have to stay down here until the doctors finish with me. I keep having sort of fits mixed with some poisoning down below ha-ha. When the fits come I am almost unconsaince [*sic*] with something coming upon me, cannot speak proper words or read them, it is a nightmare of muddle of words and frightful bells ringing and unknown crowds crying out advice, warnings, etcetera that I cannot understand, or when sanity returns remember. I am now with two doctors and have to go at once to a third who is a specialist as soon as possible. When the doctors have spent ages and ages and mornings and mornings and afternoons and afternoons, dear, stick with sticks and glass tubes and being rather sharp with steel rods, then they'll know what's the matter! I'm not sure I'll be very bright ha-ha as so often I cannot speech [*sic*] properly I scramble velly velly well. Do forgive me dear John if I've been already over and over all this again and again. I hope you are beautifully happy. Love, Stevie.

MAN: The doctors diagnosed Glioblastoma, a tumour on the brain. She lost the power of speech.

    [*Pause.*]

Stevie was sixty-nine when she wrote her final poem. Unable to speak, she scrawled a circle around one word.

I feel ill. What can the matter be?
I'd ask God to have pity on me,
But I turn to the one I know, and say:
Come, Death, and carry me away.

Ah me, sweet Death, you are the only God
Who comes as a servant when he is called, you know,
Listen then to this sound I make, it is sharp,
Come Death. Do not be slow.

    [*The* MAN *remains motionless. Lights fade.*]